They say to write well, to write what you know. Well, this is what I know…

Regardless of what the day brings, live for it. Live with gratitude in your heart. Live knowing that life and love will never be perfect; learn from it. Write out and speak your words of the past but don't live in it. It is called the present for a reason. Each day is precious. Every moment is a gift. It isn't enough to just bask in the sunshine so learn how to dance in the rain, too.

With Love,

Cynthia Lee

Life, Love, Great & Unfortunate Things

Cynthia Lee

Triple Moon Publishing

ISBN: 978-0-9889955-4-3

Life, Love, Great & Unfortunate Things

Copyright © 2022 Cynthia Lee

A PLACE TO START

Of everything I have learned in my life thus
far, the one constant whether
I was seeking it or learning how to embrace
it for myself has been Love. Even
if it was simply to learn how to love myself
so that others may come along and
be able to love and cherish me the way I had
them. But, loving myself never came easy.
Something that I struggled with because
accepting myself in all of my faults and
physical imperfections was an impossible
feat for the majority of my life. Others didn't
accept me for who I was. So, I learned that I
wasn't worth accepting, let alone loving.
Never seen for what was on the inside, solely
basing who I was on the exterior. That
nerdy, beanpole girl with bad acne and
braces. My writing, my art, my compassion,
my light and love I carried within me, ready
to give to just about anyone who needed it
was never given a chance. And so, I learned

at an early age to truly believe that I was not worth acceptance in any capacity. Maybe not even the reception of love. Coming from a home where my view of love was seen through the eyes of a little girl who used her pillow each night to get lost in many dreams and Disney movies as reference, but also, as distraction from the reality of the war raging around me, a part of me wonders if I was simply doomed to never see anything differently let alone receive it. Not that my parents ever let us go feeling unloved or want for anything, but when one of them was an alcoholic for the majority of your childhood, you learn how to escape. The yelling, the screaming, the fighting and the breaking. The leaving. The hiding. The running. When your whole world exists in such a way, it cultivates the best of imaginations. My example of love in the real world was not the one of the fairy tales that I continued to hope for. And truth be told, I never knew if someone was going to leave or not; running down the stairs to never come back at the stroke of midnight.

I knew no one would ever physically hurt me but, in a sense, I still didn't feel safe back then. The worry in my eyes was another constant and visible in nearly every childhood photo. A theme that has carried on in my life in many different types of relationships whether they be romantic or not. A poignant reality I have had to face through every painful moment of my growth as a woman, is one of my recognizing that maybe what shaped me in so many positive ways, for me to be the loving, giving, genuine and resilient Soul that I am, also have attracted all of the negative situations and human beings that I have so desperately wished to avoid.
The ones who would never truly love me as I loved them, only using me for the energy I could give to them. To build them up more so than to build a life with me. Those who lied to me, cheated me or in two of my three long-term romantic relationships, cheated on me. Those who have disrespected or neglected me. Or the true-blue narcissist who found me at one of the most vulnerable

times in my life as if he was some savior, a
Knight in shining armor, only to build me up
to break me down, imprisoning me in a cycle
of mental abuse shrouded in daily self-
doubt. He was the one that broke me to my
lowest point, until he put his hands on me
and I woke up the fuck up. I've looked for
love and acceptance in so many of the wrong
places before finding it for myself. Within
myself. Because the one thing I never fully
grasped in all of that time, what I failed to
take away from every experience: that I was
love. Every fiber of my being and its sole
existence. Something far greater than
anything I was ever looking to find outside
of myself. This is my journey, my story and
why I am the way that I am. These feelings
and passion that I share with all of you, the
hopes of something greater than everything
that this heart and Soul have experienced in
this human form.

And maybe in a way, helps others to find
hope, themselves, love or to recognize a
purpose for their life that maybe they
missed, too. It isn't easy being open and
vulnerable in a world full of judgments and

fake. But here I am. Heart and Soul pouring from the fingertips of this flesh, expressed in written word. One of Life, Love, Great and Unfortunate Things.

And it is my honor to share it all with you.

WHAT'S A LIFE-TIME?

Maybe we all just want someone who is
going to be obsessed with us for more than
three weeks, three months or 13 years.
Are we just fools for craving a lifetime?

CASTING SHADOWS OVER MY LIGHT

You think you know me. Who I am and what's buried deep within these bones. Truth is, very few do. Very few ever will. Not until we live in a world where people value hearts and souls over bodies. Those that do are the ones that are every piece of love and stardust I am made of. The deepest parts of myself I keep reserved for those willing to see my light, not just my exterior. Much of which comes out in my writing in various ways without giving too much away: raw and from the most vulnerable places. Humans have shown me, many times in my life, their shallowness and inability to see me for who I am or to merely show a willingness to grow with me. New souls casting shadows over the light of my old. A familiar scene for many, I know. Just know that not everyone deserves every piece of stardust that you are. Not everyone deserves to know every scar. Not everyone finds beauty in them. And not everyone deserves to know every bit of the love you carry within you that you so willingly give; all that you are and the only thing you know how to be. The ones that do, they will make the effort and show you why you should share all if it with them.

HOPE'S QUEEN

I am nothing if not a wild heart,
staring into hope's eyes while never
knowing what it is like to be
someone's Queen.
Forever leading a solo pack,
only to find toads who would never
turn into Princes, and Princes
who could never be Kings.

TOO MUCH & NEVER ENOUGH

I go to bed in the evenings without a good
night.
I wake up every day without a good
morning. Waking alone.
Going through all my days without an I love
you.
Celebrate each holiday without a single gift.
Light the candles on my own birthday cake
as I have for the last nine years.
Through tears. Get dressed up for myself not
some big to do.
Sit at tables for two leaving the empty chair.
Wait staff asking if anyone was to be there.
Friday nights I have nowhere but home to
be.
Love-seats at the movies holding only me.
Nobody to ask how my day was at its end.
In my nights I imagine better and pretend.
On adventures there is no one in my
passenger's seat.
The journey would be far more complete.

Meant to be shared.
I enjoy the space that we all at times need.
Some moments alone are a powerful place to
be.
But this life of being too much yet never
enough is for the birds.
Not me.

STUDENT OF THE BLUE FLAME

She's never truly been taken. Forever having
to teach a man how to touch her. Not just
physically, but to touch the very essence that
created her. Every bit of stardust that makes
her who she is; every side of her be it her
wings, her horns or her fins. She is no
teacher. And she's never desired to be. For
what she craves is deeper, darker, lighter
and as a pupil; a student eager to learn the
language of only one. One who understands
hers. Mind. Body. Soul. A million breaths
fanning the flames of her temple. A place to
be properly worshipped. She aches to study
not only what it feels like to have her heart
and her very Soul swept off the fucking
floor, but to know what it is to be a body
consumed. Carried to the Moon and the stars
by way of what he innately already knows of
her. And in all of the ways that for a moment

make her forget where she is and who she is.
Over the top from hips to finger tips, until
the only sounds are her lips, screaming his
name. She doesn't have to teach him a damn
thing. He already knows everything they
didn't: She's not the woman you light fires
for, she's the one you burn with.

GET ME OR DON'T

A man once asked me," How do I get a woman like you?"

I politely smiled and said, "You either get me, or you don't."

There is no in-between.

WHAT INTRIGUES ME

As an over-thinker who spends 90% of her time learning about and contemplating the world, the universe, hearts and souls and the more unique and rare people, places and things, those others fail to see, that's what intrigues me.

Everything wild, rare and beautiful.

BREAKING MOLDS

Whatever mold they created for humans,
it's a good thing there are souls that come
into this world and break it.
Truthfully, I don't care to know what this
fucked up world would be like without
them.
They are art, music, love, light, passion and
fire.
Pure Soul, with a side of coffee and curse
words.
And they are some of the most beautiful
creatures you will lay eyes upon,
for not just what they are on the outside.
But you already know you are the presence
of greatness long before that.
You don't just see their soul, you feel it.

CAN'T BREAK ME

They've thrown stones.
Kicked me when I've already been down.
Only to take the final shot,
expecting that to be the kill.
They may have hurt me.
Leaving behind a scar or a bruise.
But never could they permanently break me.
I never stayed down for a long.
I've never been a glass house.
And I never will be.

DEATH OF THE EGO

Strength is not hiding what's inside.
The expression of human emotion and being
able to talk about what's
killing you on the inside is not weakness of
Woman nor Man.
Being open, truthful and doing the work is
where the true strength lies.
Destroy the notion that being cold and
detached is stronger.
It's a cop-out.
Most people will never truly know the
damage they have done to another person
until they themselves experience it.
The most terrifying thing to be in a world
full of judgments and fake is to be
vulnerable.
But it is the only way to be true to yourself.

NARCISSIST YOU

You belong in a place I'd rather not name.
A predator preying on vulnerable women
like I was.
Fooling me into submission with false
promises of love.
Something you do not possess and have no
comprehension of.
Erecting a tower of terror around me based
on nothing but lies.
Your manipulation and your cruelty well
hidden behind those Devilish eyes. Yet I still
wondered what had happened in your
life to make you this way. It is a sadness.
But I am angry.
And all I can say to now is that you'll need
far more than all of the naked bodies in the
world that you strip the very Souls from to
save you.
As if saving you, is even a thing that
anything in existence could ever do.

DEARLY BELOVED, WE ARE GATHERED HERE TODAY

Life isn't always the piece of art we envision
it to be.
One of the continuous dopamine and
serotonin boosts of eternal joy.
Sometimes, it's the complete and utter
depletion of it from existence.
Devastating.
Heartbreaking.
Really fucking sad.
And in a time when everything is readily at
your fingertips with the miniature
computers we hold in the palm of our hands,
the true weapons of mass destruction,
it's easier to push away than to move
towards the reality of your own life.
Toward the good things you have in it.
Toward people that are there because they
want to be a part of it.
We find ourselves staring at a false reality
for so long, it then becomes more
sought after than anything real.

More so than all of the magic that exists
within this beautiful, but cruel world.
Instead of grounding ourselves with the true
Earth on which we stand or with the
Souls that exist in this time and space, to
listen to our own heartbeats drumming in
tune with whatever level we are in vibration
with we find ourselves unable to disconnect
long enough to tip the scales of balance back.
Our own bodies now incapacitated,
struggling each day we breathe, to return to
an ideal level of homeostasis.
And as you find yourself dazed and
confused, lost, bleeding out just barely
standing in the middle of a room screaming
with no to hear you, only then do you realize
that this is a fate born at the mercy of your
own self-destructive devices.
Everything you are, pushed onto a path not
lined with the gold or silver or the
platinum you dreamed of setting foot upon.
It is one lined with the shards of regret that
fool you into thinking they are
shimmering diamonds. And only because
the light above that feels as if you can no

longer reach it, shines down upon all of them, blinding you from the truth of what they are.

And leaving you feeling as though you have nowhere else to look than down at your own two feet. But as from all darkness, comes light. The one thing this illusion will show you if you are open enough for your vision to behold it. And if you are strong enough to keep looking above rather than below, even just one small glimpse at a time until your eyes adjust once again to the Sun, the path beneath you will change.

It is in that moment you stop desperately searching for what it was that brought you here in the first place, that you will find your way.

You will find everything you have longed for.

All that is meant for you.

And it will find you before there is nothing left to find.

LOVE

Love,
to know Love
and to truly know it,
is to know that the
only thing it will
ever ask for in return,
is Love.

LOVE PART 2

Of everything I've learned in decades of my
journey in this thing called life, there is only
one thing that can shut out evil, darkness,
transcend time and be spoken in every
language without saying a word.
It is expressed through us, our passions,
creativity, music, nature and Earth's energy.
And it is the one special gift that we as
humans have the largest capacity inside of
us for, that at the center of everything else, is
what life is truly all about.

Love.

It is what makes it worth living.
And no matter what you believe in
spiritually, it was what was truly intended
for us as our existence on this Earth comes
from it as we are the embodiment of it. Even
when we are lost or become so distant from
it while on our individual paths, it is still
there.

We are surrounded by it. It never leaves. It carries us through it all.

It catches us when we fall and we feel like letting go. And we are never alone because of it, always right in front of us in various ways even when we are too far into our dark places to see.

The mind is a place easily influenced by darkness in all forms; fear, temptation, self-doubt, limiting beliefs, manipulation and uncertainty.

Too much over-thinking can lead us down the most destructive paths against ourselves and others.

But the heart it is pure light.

Lead with it in all that you say and do in this life, choose it first, and you can never go wrong.

Lead with love, all it stands for and you will never be lost to the darkness for too long.

MONEY

Money isn' t everything.
But Love is.
Some say it isn't enough.
I disagree.
If you have it everything else follows.
When you have it, you have everything.

FALLING LIKE THE STARS

I'm ready to be loved in a way that would
make the Moon blush.
And I'm ready to love in a way that the stars
will continuously fall from the sky around
us. Until each, our final breath.

A MOMENTARY REPREIEVE

If I could trace every bit of ink on your skin
with my fingertips, caressing away every
scar you carry hidden beneath them,
offering a momentary reprieve from your
awareness that they exist, I would.
And I would do it every night until each of
your scars was replaced with the love you
have always, deserved.
Your ink reborn, becoming something of
only Love and Art.

NOTHING MORE NOTHING LESS

You can be nothing more
than you are.
But, nothing less.
And truth be told,
I wouldn't want you,
any other way.

A SOUL THAT FEELS TOO MUCH

For so many years of my life I wondered if I
was the problem.
If something was wrong with me.
But now as I look around me, I see so much
wrong within the world.
Then it hit me.
Maybe it's just difficult to exist in a world
that isn't built to support a heart and Soul
that feels too much.
So deeply, everything.

TRAVELERS

We are all just travelers in this life here on
Earth.
For it is only one of the stops between here
and the Sun, the Moon and the stars;
between all of the universes and beyond.

TRAVELERS PART 2

It isn't possible to make a masterpiece out of
everything, but you can create one out of
your own life.
We are all travelers on a journey here that
can end at any moment.
So, speak your mind.
Tell people how you feel.
Love hard.
Have that second piece of cake.
Go on an adventure with someone just for
adventures sake.
Share space with those worthy of it.
Connect with those who get you.
Let go of those who don't and disturb your
peace.
Forgive others for yourself and forgive
yourself.
Do the things that scare you most.
Don't live with reckless abandon, but just
live.
Live with integrity, values and respect but
don't be so tightly bound that you are

incapable of enjoying a moment or three.
You never know what will be unless you let
it be.
Embrace every great possibility of this life
before it runs out.
Hold nothing back, ever.
No regrets, traveler.
No regrets.

NO MATTER WHAT

No matter what, be honest, open and
authentic.
Even if it isn't the best side of you for the
world to see.
We all have our strengths, weaknesses, good
sides, bad ones that need work; the sides
that our personal life experiences have
shaped over the years.
Sometimes we don't know the best way to
deal with that.
But that's normal, that's human.
As no matter what you face in your life, how
judged you feel or misjudged, how sad,
hurt or angry you feel or maybe even how
broken inside by whatever you are hurt by,
it is okay to be real about it. Just remember
that time, albeit it moves more slowly than
we want in moments of great pain and
faster than we want in moments of intense
joy, it will eventually heal and change all.
Time is the greatest truth you can never run
from as it forces you to face what little bit of

it you have on this Earth.
Your energy should not be wasted for a
second on that which harms you or doesn't
light your Soul on fire!
It reminds you to breathe deep and exhale,
forgive yourself and let go of that which
does not serve you.
And even when we don't see it, in those
moments we feel so trapped in the negative
spaces we didn't create and have zero
control over in this roller-coaster ride we call
life, remember that the truth always finds
a way to prevail. Whether it be your truth or
the absolute, irrefutable truth.
It is the ultimate ingredient to loving
ourselves from within and in turn, the only
true means of having the ability to genuinely
and selflessly project love and light to the
world, and onto others.

PURE INTENTIONS

I told her she could ask me anything.
And so, she asked me, "If you don't believe
in the whole, you get what you give thing
anymore, why do you do it?"

The answer was simple.
And sure, one of which simply because I
love to see people light up.
To smile with a full heart.

But the brutal truth is what became my
single answer, "Because when you know
what it is like to feel unloved, you never
want anyone you care about to ever feel that
way."

And she just smiled at me, as if she didn't
know what to say. I am not a pessimist by
any means. Quite the opposite actually.
I still want to believe in karma, the threefold
rule and that all of the good energy and love
we give, comes back to us. In this life or the

next. But I've learned that the root of all disappointment in this life is expectation. Of which having none not only simplifies a whole lot, more importantly, it allows for only the purest of intentions.

TO FIND YOU

And as I watched your lips move with every
word you were able to speak, it was your
eyes that stole the show.
The captivating windows full of all that you
are.
Every bit of hope and Soul.
I've been lost before.
A scary place to be.
But lost in your eyes, your smile, your heart
and your Soul is the only lost place I want to
be.
I never understood why.
Why I had been played for a fool some many
times.
Heartbroken. Lied to. Cheated. Mistreated.
Never truly appreciated.
I thought to give up after the last time.
To that day you came, still wondering why
life led me where it did.
But now I know exactly why.
To find you.

SHADOWS BE LIGHT

I told myself many times of how guarded I
was by a wall of shadows that others had
built. One so strong that even with its small
cracks begging to open up to the world,
not a Soul was getting in.

Then there YOU were.

Pouring your heart and Soul out for anyone
who is brave enough to open up their
wounds to your words. And so, I told
myself to be brave. I opened up my wounds.

Then there YOU were.

And before I could open and close my eyes
fast enough to even see you do it, the
indomitable light that you are flooded in
through the cracks.
It was a light that no wall of shadows could
ever withstand.

Then there YOU were.

So here I am. This time, not questioning whether or not you will stay.

EVERYONE HAS A STORY

Everyone has a story.
Find those who want nothing more
than to be a part of yours.
You are far too much magic to be
confined to one book, one world.
So don't limit yourself to one.

KISS ME & TELL ME YOUR SECRETS

And if the world were ending tomorrow,
I'd ask you about every last piece of Stardust
that created your Soul.
Keep me in your embrace until the flames
come to destroy us all.
Kiss me softly and lie to me, tell me
everything will be all right.
But not before every last one of your truths
are told.

DROWINING IN YOUR OCEAN

Some people dive in.
I used to.
After hitting my head on the bottom so
many times,
now I only dip my toes in.
Rarely do I put my feet in the water all the
way first.
Especially when the water isn' t warm
enough.
The instant chill a warning to go, to stay
away.
They' ve been the Pacific North.
But you are The Gulf of Mexico.
Your ocean I would put my feet in, then my
legs.
My hands.
My chest.
My heart over my head.
Maybe I would drown in it.
Only coming up for air to keep living for
you.

ALL YOURS

And so here I am wishing you were holding
me close tonight. Maybe you are.
No one has sparked a passion for all of the
things I had long forgotten about in the last
seven years of my life's ups and downs.
Especially in love.
Nor had they so quickly sparked a desire
and need for embrace as I had been
content on giving to myself. Loving me for
the first time in a long time.
But somehow you came along, shattering my
own self-limiting beliefs of what I was
capable of opening up to in my life again
and what I truly deserved.
You healed me. But you already knew that.
I don't know as much about your heart as I
would like to, but I see a reflection of
something inside of me, in you. Something
you feel too. And the parts of you that I have
seen and felt are the same as me.
A wholeness that brings me such comfort yet
a certain restlessness all the same.

My Soul craves yours. I crave you.
What I saw, what I felt, I will probably
always want to have more of.
We joke of only going away when one tells
the other to "fuck off" damn well knowing
and citing how neither of us will ever do it. I
know it is something you cannot fathom nor
can I. I will never leave you. I believe forever
does exits.
I know our mirrors reflect each other so
much that maybe it's a terrifying feeling
for two hearts that have been betrayed and
left behind as ours have. To fully be
vulnerable with anyone after time and time
again, everyone leaves. Showing us their
faults as much as our own. But for once, I
find myself begging the Universe to
withhold the next cosmic cruel joke to play
on me that would be just another in a
lifelong game of which I tire of playing. A
game at which it never seems that I can win.
My lightness, my dark and my intense
giving nature comprised solely of pure love,
forever scaring people away. Even the ones
who say they are ready for all of it.

And it pains me more than you know, to
understand how this has filled many pages
of your own book. But that is past. Not the
future. Something that you have helped me
to realize and let go of. For I will never again
hold onto these notions of mine.
Something that I am grateful beyond words
and forever indebted to you for.
And so, it is my great wish that maybe I
would be able to offer you the same peace as
you have bestowed upon me. I am grateful
and my heart is full simply for the fact that
you are living and breathing. For knowing of
your very existence and you knowing of
mine. I needed someone like you and then
you came along. There you were telling me
of how I was "something else" yet I had the
same thought in my mind, incapable of
escaping my lips or my fingertips, before
they did yours.
I don't know how to properly express to you
what it all means to my heart and Soul.
But I try.
So here I write forever to the heavens for you
choosing to be a part of my existence too.

However that may be. Just know that you'll never be too much for me. I will never get enough of you. You forever have my love, my light, the reciprocity of appreciation and a home built by Moon dust and Sun rays if you ever so wanted to claim it. A home in a space that others never bothered to truly understand. One rarely seen let alone open in a way for them to be close enough to feel in all of the ways that you already have been privy to. You needn't ever ask if you can hold me.
The answer will always be the same. You may keep me close on any night or any day. Always. Forever.
And I will continue to be, "Too fucking good to you" just please, be gentle with me.
And if I, "Feel so fucking good to you" then feel me. All you want or ever need to. I will never allow you to run dry. And if ever again you find yourself uttering those words that I have burned into my memory by the sheer passion you speak to me with, "Yours. All yours. You're all mine" mean it because I won't see you as anything less. And I will be all of your everything. All yours. Every. Part.

UNCOMPLICATED

She is simple. It is you who complicates her. Because she shares her feelings like an open book. She communicates because she does not believe in games, especially the waiting ones. She asks for very little. And she prefers action over empty words. As she has faced many broken promises. The lies that others have fed her. She seeks peace. Nothing else. So, if she becomes angry there is a genuine reason. Just as if she becomes silent there is one too. One that without a word says you have lost her. So, if she means something, tell her. Don't leave her thinking and wondering. Don't leave her guessing. Don't leave her feeling like she isn't anything. What she feels, she will believe to be true.

A SMALL PIECE OF FOREVER

There is no touch for me other than your
tender caress.
To fly me so high in the sweet ecstasy of
your essence.
One kiss is all it takes to strip the air from
my lungs,
to fill them all the same.
One look is all it takes to be still this
devastated heart.
In your space is where I feel safe,
in this small piece of forever,
With you.

SELF-DOUBT

The things we are afraid we are not,
or what we fear we can or cannot be,
that's everyone's fight.
You are not alone.
You are more than enough.
And you have more to offer than you know.
It just takes the right person to see it.
To appreciate it.
And to tell you every day.
Forever.

WRITTEN IN THE STARS

Maybe it was written in the Stars,
sealed with a kiss from the Moon
and set ablaze by the fire of the Sun
that our paths would cross.

HOLD ME CLOSE UNDER THE MOON & I'LL CARRY YOU TO THE STARS

I've chosen myself over and over again but,
I've always left room to choose others too.
A rare find in these days in a world full of
arrogance.
Apes with ego trips.
The space I carry within this heart, this Soul,
just full enough to comfort so many.
But I hold no delusions of my own capacity.
One cannot save the world with a single
beating heart.
Trying to do so will leave you eternally
pouring from a hollow chalice.
Balance is required.
Many have taken with no reciprocity,
yet I've retained just enough to save myself
when needed.
Each time binding every fractured piece that
I could pick up, clutching them to my chest;
all of the pieces that had fallen in the
wake of my holding too firmly, to the jagged

edges of others.
A single beating heart cannot fix them, if it is
not their own.
A dispiriting lesson to learn.
Especially for an Empath.
So now, the light of the Moon, the Sun and
the Stars keep me on my path to all of my
dreams.
While Earth, Air, Water and Fire continue to
evolve within this old Soul.
My heavy wings keep me safe, bound only
to me; protecting this bleeding heart from
every dagger thrown in my direction.
But what good are wings if you don't open
them to fly to the heavens now and again,
to the Moon and the Stars, basking in all that
they are. Or to hover near the Sun when you
need to feel the warmth that others fail
to return to you.
Or to open, allowing yourself to love again,
to hold close someone who will hold you the
same. Just as a single beating heart cannot
save the world, a single pair of wings cannot
carry it. But these wings, they're not only
strong enough now to open and carry one
more, but light enough for us both to fly.

THE PROMISE UNDER THESE WINGS

At sunset I looked around and noticed a
solemn tree on the beach.
Resurrected by rocks and sand, surrounded
by families and lovers laughing, some
walking hand-in-hand.
But even bearing witness to their genial
energy, he was lonely. Left with no choice
other than to wait for something far greater
than he was, while seizing the last of the
day's light. He would soon be dismantled by
the sea during the night, carried adrift
by the current to an unmarked grave.
His spirit knowing what humans did not,
that these well intended stones
left to protect him did not bear the weight of
water.
So, I moved closer.
Softy, and with extra care as I made my
presence known.
But he already knew I was there long before
the thought crossed my mind.

In that acknowledgment of my intentions, of who I was and why I had come, I caught more than a mere glimpse of all that he was and ever had been. And it was his everything that not only kissed my skin to touch my essence, but held me in its arms comprised of only pure love and genuine embrace.

My heart forthwith no longer at war and my Soul fed.

Both had been undernourished for so long they had fallen too close to the Angel of Death's blade. Much like he was ever so near being swept away by an unforgiving tide.

Every night, he faced the wrath of the same current that I too no longer had the fight left in me to swim against.

I hadn't opened my wings in so long, I wondered if I could even fly.

And it was in that moment he granted me a piece of his serenity.

One born of the acceptance of all of the ethereal things in this plane that could not be physically held.

He was a quiet calm to wash over my

wounded Soul and a weathered heart.
Love and light.
As I too was the embodiment of love meant
to heal, water for thirsts needing to be
quenched, and the earth of which he needed
to bury sturdy roots in order to stay here.
As we sat there to watch the sun slip from
view, I could feel his fear of the dark fall
away. Descending to the depths of hell
where such fears belong, giving rise to a new
night offering the shelter he longed for.
One bathed in the tranquility of the full
Moon's radiance and guarded by
the wings I had until now, kept closed and
bound tightly to myself.
Even on the days they fell heavy upon my
shoulders.
Opening them now, a promise that he would
never again be lonely, no more humans
piling on stones in a feeble attempt to stop a
lifetime of the only fate he ever knew.

TO CRAVE YOU

I woke up this morning and my first thought
was you.
But I didn't want to be overbearing. So here I
sit.
I feel you now, like you told me to do. It feels
good.
It is indeed a strange feeling to love you as I
do when I barely know you. The foreign
sensation of how I crave you.
When I have not truly craved a Soul in this
way for some time.
To be near you. To touch you. And if I could
right now, it would feel like sticking my
finger in an electrical socket.
Or at least as I would imagine that would
feel like.
It's how your energy hits me with every
letter you've written or any piece you have
sent as it rests in my hands.
So much so that when the day comes for you
to physically hold me, hold me firmly when
my feet fail beneath me.

I'm trying so hard to hold back for now, for reasons that I cannot explain. Not even to myself. Because truth be told, I don't want to. And maybe I know deep down, I don't have to.

LONGING FOR YOUR LOVE

I catch my breath by gazing upon the stars in
the sky, making wishes consumed by the air.
They beg of the moon as my hands rise
above my shoulders.
To pull it down to earth.
Down to me.
To swaddle my Soul like a blanket of
consolation.
To soothe this longing for you.
For your love.
I've never been afraid to unfold the mystery
of this heart I carry. Ad nauseum, giving it
the third degree.
Yet it is still a Pandora's box screaming to be
opened by those gallant enough to be hold it.
The treasures inside nothing of physical or
emotional curses.
Just seductive mysteries and unrequited
love.
Love I would give anything to give to you.

UNREQUITED LOVE

I don't know how or why, and it scares me.
By all logic and reason, it should.
My heart is crossing swords with my mind.
When I wake you are there. But you're not.
I've never touched your skin with these
temperate hands but felt your Soul with
them.
And a beating heart that is still sore.
Yet it heals gently and violently in the same
beat.
You teach me of varied truths and dreams
that my bones hold.
They carry you with them.
Maybe they always have, long before my lips
could ever moan your name.
Being born of the moon and stars, the same
reflective light as I am, how could they not.
Telling the story of an elemental love.
And on the days all I can do is feel you,
your essence finds me in the sunshine and
whispers in my ear with the ocean breeze.
And it is on those days I beg myself to hold

these feelings back. Something this
boundless heart knows nothing of how.
Maybe you could tell me how you do it.
I've told myself I'd never feel that again.
A prisoner to the broken promises of
someone else.
Looking for what I used to believe I so lost in
one, in everyone I meet.
Searching for the fire of the sun.
But maybe fire is not what we need.
As those who play with fire are destined to
be burned.
Leaving a pile of ash in the wake.
What Great and Unfortunate Things I have
held onto in my life, to be cursed by an
earthly existence without eternal embrace.
Forever believing my feet will always be
bare, torn by the jagged rocks and sharp
stones of unrequited love.
Then you show up.
And suddenly all of the Stardust in the
galaxy and the light of the Moon rest at my
feet. Your soul perusing my own through
those blue windows.
A sensation of childlike wonder, wholeness

and care.
The absolute essence of all that you are.
The life you breathe into my lungs, the all-encompassing perfect storm.
A calming air followed by a rush of chaos and calm again.
I don't know what to do with all of these emotions inside, but I've never been good at concealing them.
I don't know where they will lead me.
It scares me.
But not knowing, scares me more.
And so, I offer but one final thought;
Maybe the Moon does not need the Sun as they can never share the same space in the sky for long. Maybe it needs another Moon to exist in that space in which it will never leave.

CONTENT

I couldn't be happier.
For you to see me.
For you to feel me.
It is magic.
Something outside of Space and Time.
All that you can and cannot be.
All that I can and cannot be.
The closeness.
The tension.
Worth the wait.
Worth every moment.

TOUCH ME

Yes. Touch me in all the places no one has
ever touched. Put your hands to my
chest and reach inside. I want you to feel me
in all the ways others have failed to.
Go deep and I will share with you all of my
secrets.

SAPPHIRE SOUL

As intoxicating to me is the scent of the rain
the moment it falls upon parched Earth,
is your light. The colors that surround you.
The beauty in your eyes whenever I behold
them, your sapphire Soul, one of wisdom,
royalty, and divine favor.
You are a soothing balm for the heart, one of
healing, happiness, the gem of all gems.
And in your presence, I am destroyed.
No chance do I stand to remain upright on
my own two feet against your desire.
Your embrace. For they are enough to
capture every last star from the sky,
pulling them down from the Heavens to
Earth.
Your gravity pulling the Moon and the Sun
down behind them.
The depth you possess, like a magnet that
pulls me closer to wait another day for you.
For no matter where I am in this time and
space, I crave you.
Feeling your passion when you feel me,

strengthening my connection to you.
To this very Universe.
Your fire when see me.
Your touch when your energy reaches mine.
And when you put your hand to my chest to
reach inside, only you know how to go just
deep enough that I will tell you all of my
secrets. Barring all reserve.
My cravings for you go beyond your body,
they go beyond my own and in a way that
you will always be enough. Yet I will never
be satiated. Never close enough. Never
getting enough, of you.
But for now, if I were granted a moment to
hold your face in my hands, I would spend
forever searching what's between them.
Learning you. Holding you in all of the ways
that others have failed to. Or for as long as
you would allow me to.
As I know that your lips always have a way
of finding mine if I gaze too long.
They'll be kissing me softly, then harder
with a hint of your velvet tongue.
It is here that I feel what you feel.
No longer do I hold back these words

knowing you do not want me to.
So, wrap me in your arms and I with trace a
path down to interlacing fingers, to
unwavering connection.
All parts acquiesced to all of me inside of
you, and all of you inside of me.

THIS LONGING

And this morning when I woke up to the
sun's radiant light dancing across to my
forehead, like the feathers of your fingertip's
caress, I knew it was you.
I could feel you there in the warmth of a new
day.
Holding me.
Touching me.
In every way.
I could feel your lips as if they were really
fixed upon mine.
A welcomed sensation of embrace.
Knowing damn well that if my lips were to
touch yours just once, that will never be
enough to quench this desire for all that you
are.
Waking up to this beautiful dream that is
you.
But you're real.
And just knowing you exist is everything.
This longing and need to be chosen.
Taken. To feel you inside. Held close.

Close enough to reach into your Soul.
And to feel your heart beat someday, only
for me.
Mine already beats only for you.

ALWAYS WITH YOU

And even on the days you can't hear me,
I hope you feel me.
I'm here.
I'm with you.
And I hope that feeling comforts you,
bringing a smile to your heart today.
And in that energy,
I hope you feel so loved as to not feel so
alone.

TOO BEAUTIFUL FOR WORDS

And if so, they asked me,
"What is the most beautiful part of you?"
How do I answer?
To choose one single part?
I could say your ocean blues as they pull the
breath from my lungs the way the tide pulls
the sand out to Sea.
I could say the words you speak or the
sound of your voice singing its heart song.
For the world goes silent around me,
every time you do.
And so, I could say your lips for every time
they move, I yearn to kiss them.
And sure, I could say your strong body.
A work of art with all of its scars.
This embrace and desire and protection I feel
from it, whenever you hold me close.
Wrapped around me and entwined with me.
Or would the most beautiful part be that
space in the middle of your chest, where you
pull me in to rest my head as you stroke my
hair.

Maybe I could say your smile.
For when you do it brings a warmth to my
heart and a light to a world that hardly
deserves you.
So how do I answer them?
An impossible task, if ever there were one.
But if I had to, there would be this.
The light and the dark.
The inside and the outside.
Every bit of the old Soul you carry within
you.
Too beautiful for words.
All of it. All of you.
Every. Part.

FILL YOUR SPACE

Sometimes
you must fill the space
you rest your head, with
beautiful things to keep
your dreams alive
and the nightmares
at bay.

TO FEEL SAFE

All we really want is to know
we are safe and protected.
Not just by the words we are
trusting in, but by the hands
of those who speak them.

ALPHA

A protection over my shoulder so close that
even at a distance I can feel his claims
staked.
One that is his right alone if he so chooses to
take.
Eyes burning like wild blue flame, heated
breath upon my neck at the curve.
A force beyond ancient in spirit, innate and
even primal.
Beyond any amount of space and time.
As even at a distance I can feel his strong
essence positioned in the wind behind each
step I take.
Before me. Beside me. Behind me.
More power over me.
Yet unafraid of the power I hold.
As mirrors. Equals. The Same.
Howling at the Moon, that low growl, that
bark and that bite of his words are enough to
be the ruin of a world, or the ruler of one.
I just hope that when he comes, we don't
burn it all down.

NEVER WILL I EVER

I will never stop appreciating you
and showing you how much you mean in
this world. But also, in my world.
And I won't leave, unless you do.

LOVE IS ART

Love is art.
And music.
That something that evokes every wild
and uninhibited human emotion,
encompassed by the human experience.

GOODNIGHT MOON

For when my home claims me,
there will be no desire or need for anyone
else to see me.
As long as he does, the rest of this digital
world can fall away and disappear.
For in this beautiful space between us as we
live our lives, I am happy. For no true spaces
felt that all.
Goodnight Moon.
And all of your stars

TO TELL YOU THE TRUTH

To tell you the truth,
no one has ever done to me what you do.
So, have all of me.
All of me.
I'm at your door.
Open it.
All you have to do is let the light inside.

ONLY YOU

It's always an ache for you.
Only you.
For the moment I can look you in the eyes.
To touch you, to feel just how real you are.
To wrap my arms around you, my head to
your heart.
Holding you, holding me.
But not just our bodies.
Our interlocking hands.
The warm embrace felt by entwined fingers.
The connection.
That single touch before finding your lips.
That longing for.
Only you

TALKING TO THE MOON

All of the colors cast lucent shadows upon
your words.
The music of your heart rising above me.
A cherished melody echoing within these
walls.
Laying here under many Moons, I am
restless in my pursuit of tranquil sleep, to
find you at your Castle in the sky.
If I could only find the prowess to speak
these words, knowing all too well if you
stood before me my lips would fail to
produce them.
Yet souls like ours don't need words to speak
in a language known by few.
For even if you cannot hear them,
may my essence embrace you in these
daydreams.
Entwined with your own, when it calls for
you during the night.
Whether it finds you or not is mere
conjecture in my mind.
I wish I knew.

All I do know is this love I hold,
is for you.

A SCAR & A SKELETON

Forgive me for my self-doubt when it creeps
in; the one that challenges my usual air of
confidence. That of my knowing how I am as
worthy of you, as I am worthy to myself.
Good enough for you, the same way I am
good enough for myself. When everyone
you've ever wanted to see all of you and still
want to keep you as their own, leaves for
someone else, the feeling that you won't be
for the one you want most is a ghost never
too far behind you. A scar and a skeleton.
One that falls out of a locked closet from
time to time. I hope you see all of me and
stay. I never want you to leave. But I do
crave to know what it is like for that ghost
to, and for that scar to finally feel beautiful.

SOMETIMES BRAVE

Sometimes I am brave.
But sometimes,
I am really fucking terrified.
I guess that is the consequence
of a Soul and a body that
craves so much more than this.

BEING PRESENT

I am trying more to be present.
To focus more on what I do have versus that
which I do not.
We only find ourselves stuck in our own
minds when we focus on what is not sitting
right in front of our own two eyes or to be
held in our own two hands.
It is not easy some days.
Sometimes I feel like I self-sabotage like all
humans do.
And seemingly every time when things are
good.
And so, I wonder why, with no good
explanation.
Except maybe that's what happens when you
become accustomed to things being so bad,
for far too long.

LOVE'S GHOST

There's still that part of me, that in the
silence, tells me the lies of my past. I don't
live in that space, but recognize the thoughts
as a part of what's shaped me; helping me to
grow to be the woman I am now. Who I
continue to grow to be, how I love and
where all the love I have to give comes from.
A woman who shows a resilient and
adventurous heart, adapting to the types of
adversity faced where I've watched others
crumble under the weight; retreating to
what's known. A place of comfortability.
One of settling for less than what truly
represents their eccentric Soul. Settling for
far less than what they deserve. And
sometimes, of straight abuse, cruelty and
manipulation. But I'd be lying to you if I told
you I hadn't ever done the same. I have
crumbled. Settled. Forgiven abuse and
manipulation, all in the name of one-sided
love. All because l yearned to be loved when
I didn't even love myself enough to know

that none of it was right, back then. So, it is
no surprise to me as to why I found myself
there at different points in my life, especially
as a kid growing up thinking that love meant
screaming, fighting, breaking shit and
hiding. It's a fucking dark place no man nor
beast will ever again hold me hostage to, any
more than I will ever again bind myself to,
by way of my own chains. Being vulnerable
in love has been one of the most terrifying
things for me in my adult life. Mainly
because not once in my life have I ever been
shown why I should have been. And so that
is why, in silence some days, I find peace
and happiness. While in others, I find the old
skeletons of self-doubt and uncertainty
where I desperately crave the warmth of
reassurance. Those rare times when I am
incapable of reassuring myself. Something
no man nor woman can do when it comes to
what resides in the human hearts of others.
And no matter how innately connected we
are as Souls who feel things more deeply
than most, we are no mind readers. For no
matter how much you've overcome, no

matter what's in your heart, your Soul, what
you know to be true, how much you have
learned to let go of and move forward in
your life and in love, confidence isn't
possible every moment of the day. Especially
when it comes to a love you've read about in
fairy-tales or dreamt of to keep your demons
away. One you will cherish more than the air
in your lungs, the heart beating in your chest
to keep you alive, yet all the while preparing
for it to leave because that's all you have ever
known. That self-fulfilling prophecy that can
only be destroyed by faith in love, despite of
your past. I've grown to never doubt what I
am capable of, what I am worthy of and
what I have to offer not only this world but
to he who chooses to stay in mine. None of
them have, but I'm glad they didn't. Because
it led me to you. And although I have faith, I
am a flawed human. So, all I can ask is to be
forgiven when my insecurity in love shows
up in the form of a ghost that haunts me
from time to time. I can speak to it calmly
until I know what it wants, making its
presence less known to me. But it is when
you wrap me in the comfort of your words,

that it leaves.

LET IT BE

The past is the past, so let it be.
I cannot change it.
And no future for anyone can be guaranteed.
Focus on the past,
and I will forever suffer the anxiety
that comes along with it.
The worry.
The over-thinking.
The throw back to its negative loop.
A place I refuse,
I refused to go back to.

COLD NIGHTS

It's nights like these when
it's a little too silent.
A little too loud.
A little too lonely.
It's in these moments I wish
I had you here the most.

WICKED GAME

It isn't always easy to be happy or brave.
It's heavy when you feel like a ghost.
You tire of being told how much the world
needs your light as you are starving for it.
With no one around to show you they do.
You are so full of love as you are crawling on
your hands and knees through an endless
desert, lips cracking and throat parched for
it.
Giving all the love you can to yourself is
meant to always carry you through the
darkest of nights.
A notion the idealist in me carries while
fighting with the realist in me who calls
bullshit.
Humans were not created to exist only in
this way, just as souls were never created
whole so they could be a part of life's wicked
game of hide and seek for its missing parts.
And in the moments you once again stop
dreaming long enough to see no one around
you, you can love yourself as much as you

want.
Be as grateful for everything else you would
gladly give up for something else or
someone else, as much as you want.
There is still that ache growing with each
year that passes, one that ends each day to
remind you that somehow, you're still alive
and able to touch the living world; but only
as a ghost behind a keyboard that would no
longer matter if the batteries in it died.

EXHAUSTION

You want to know the truth?
People can be exhausting at times.
That doesn't mean I love them any less.
But being lonely, that's exhausting too.
The things people don't say.
But nevertheless,
every person you encounter,
be kind and judge no one.
You have not survived through their
hardships.
You have never walked a day in their shoes.

HALO

May the sun be shining for you
today and every day,
brightening your halo as you
spread your wings and fly.

TRUE JOY

To be honest with you,
I don't believe it is possible to know true joy
until you are responsible for bringing it to
someone else's life.
Even if there is no way that they can ever
repay you.
The smallest of things can mean so much.
And not enough people pay attention to the
details.
But I do.

YOU ARE MAGIC

You are far too much magic to be half loved
or go unloved.
And if this is something you need to tell
yourself every single fucking day until you
believe it, speak the words.
Write them on every wall.

FOR WINTER

I can't believe you are really gone.
All of our memories I will carry with me.
I will carry you with me.
Until the day we meet again in heaven.
You changed lives.
You changed me.
How blessed are we to have been loved by
you?
Forever grateful.
You were Angel on Earth with wings of the
sea.
Now in heaven you can do both.
Swim and fly free.

For Winter ~Always

EVERY MOON, EVERY STAR

And if you so find something rare in this life,
in a world where so much magic is lost to a
limited view, don't just pick it up.
Hold it against the cadence of your heart
until it melds with your body in a manner of
which no man nor beast could ever strip it
away.
Breathe into it the kind of life that even death
cannot remove from your grasp.
For it is those rare treasures that are worth
far more than all of their weight in rose
colored Rhodium.
Some precious metals and jewels are far too
brilliant to only be known by an X on a map.
And that is how I see you.
As even in your darkness, you shine brighter
than every star in the night sky, of not only
our Moon but of all of the planets and their
Satellite Moons.
The seventy-nine of Jupiter.
I only know of your body and photographs
existing in a place on a map.

But I dream of someday connecting it to the
Soul you bear to me as I know maps are
meant to be followed just as treasures
are not meant to be hidden, and only the
brave will know what to do with them when
found.
I found you. And now I am brave.
And on the days you wake only to retreat to
the chest sitting beside you, to protect
yourself from your ghost or the demons
peddling fears of your past as if they are
some inevitable future for you, I am there.
The warm air you feel upon your lips,
breathing into you that same courage your
words, your heart and every last fiber of
your very existence has bestowed upon me.
You will never know another who stands
above your grave only to throw another red
rose into it as their final goodbye.
Or at least you will not know that of me.
For as long as I draw breath, they will never
seal your grave to create another X on a map
that is yearning to be found.
A treasure far too exquisite and rare to ever
again be someone else's buried memories.

YOUR HEART TO TRUST

I woke up this morning and my first thought
was of you.
But I've always been too much for everyone.
I'm trying so hard to hold back.
I wish I didn't have to.
So here I lay thinking of you.
Feeling you.
And knowing you feel me too is enough.
It feels good to be in that space.
Because I understand you differently than
others.
What a strange feeling it is to love you when
there is so much more I would like to know.
Yet I feel I know everything I need to know.
For when you know someone's heart and see
their Soul, that's the only thing you need to
know to trust.

THAT SOMETHING

There is something incredibly
sexy about this man.
His gentle Aura.
His kind Soul.
His fiery passion unafraid of depth,
power or a dirty mind.
His honesty.
His truth.
And in his excitement,
the way curse words fall from his lips.

THE CARESS OF YOUR WORDS

I've had a rough go at sleep the past couple
of nights. Uncomfortable in my skin that has
been freshly painted of beautiful things,
resting upon my shoulder. The healing. One
that always starts with the burn but ends in
comfort, embrace and the love art can bring.
If it were not for feeling you there, closing
my eyes to look into yours, to feel your touch
by way of your words, the night would yet
again have not allowed restful sleep to befall
me. Last night was the first it had, in days.
And instead of vibrant visions, dreams
played in full color upon the screens that
cover my eyes. I drifted off to your voice and
the whisper of your words. They echoed
through my sheets reaching every part of my
body, every inch of my skin, as if to be the
caress of your hands. Moving like the
gentlest ocean breeze before finding shelter
in the warmth of the sun, their usual resting
place tucked between my thighs. I could feel
your breath as each syllable rolled from your

tongue, as if each were meant to fall upon the crook of my neck. That place I imagine where you'd rest your head for a while. Your lips close enough for me to inhale each one, while replenishing it with my own in return. It's incredible how you do that; how you have that effect on me by way of spoken or written word even when I can't see your face or hold your body in real time. So eloquent, so vulnerable, so honest, raw, real, intelligent and even if not intended, sexy as fuck. It's not only your gift, one that not many can say they possess. It is but a single part of the gift that is all you; the only one I crave. One with a history I want to dive into like diving into leaves of grass, a complete understanding of distinct beauty, of you as a unified whole. Completed by the soulful depth I've forever longed for. You once told me how I was something else. Well, you sir, are something other worldly.

SEPTEMBER 23rd

I never thought I would find the courage to
write my story, let alone write the words of
my heart and soul.
Ripping it wide open for the world to see.
Some things born of every best and worst
moment of my life up to and including now.
Of life, love great and unfortunate things.
But I found my bravery as if it had always
been there wrapped in gold and laced with
fire.
I have always shared pieces of myself with
the world that I felt like it needed. But even
so, there are the deeper parts I have kept
hidden in my journals or simply as words
unspoken. Those of heartache and every
spirit crushing moment that only now do I
understand made me stronger. But on
September 23 of this year, I was finally
brave. It was the beautiful words, kind heart
and radiant Soul of a human that crossed my
path at exactly the time I needed him to, just
the day before. It was only then did the

courage to open the black box I had bound ever so tightly to my chest. And in that, a healing came. Along with the ability to not only move on, but to write the stories I was always meant to. All the while knowing those feelings have been felt, now passed and I can be remembered as nothing more than a lesson for the future. But also, to maybe help others the same way his words helped me.

This was the first thing I wrote on the first day of my eventual healing...

I'm going to keep a smile on my face.
I'm going to tell you I'm not hurting.
I'm going to tell you I'm doing just fine.
Pretending that I don't need anyone.
Acting like I've healed the parts of me afraid everyone will always leave.
I'm going to pretend I sleep as I once did.
But I barely sleep at all.
I'm going to pretend I dream as I once did.
But there are none at all. Like I don't long for you.

When I do.
I'm going to pretend I don't need that
chemistry or connection.
The kind that made my soul smile without
speaking a word.
Because who wants those kinds of things
these days.
I did. I do. But no.
I'm going to lie to myself anyway.
Every moment your voice echoes in my
head.
Every moment your touch lingers in my
heart.
I'm going to lie to myself anyway.
Until a lie becomes true.
When the truth is me missing you.

You will heal. You will move on. And one
day I promise you, you won't miss them.
You won't hurt anymore and you will be
able to make space for far better than you
ever could have imagined.

BREATH, BLOOD & BONE

When you've crossed thousands of seas
seeking a gallant shore of which to ground
yourself, many ships come and the go; as do
Siren's calls.
Enough for me to know the difference
between a beacon to get you through the
most treacherous night, an anchor for which
to rest your weary hull against a raging sea,
or a pirate ship offering nothing more than a
long walk that ends at the bottom of it,
in chains. When you have felt that the
splinters on your soles of enough wooden
boards, your feet tethered to sinking bricks,
you learn how to break free of them with just
enough time to breathe at the surface of a
new day.
Another precious moment granted; to find
my anchor.
The deep-sea never a secure place for any
ship, let alone mine.
One that knows not the same anchors of
those I pass, who are steady in one place

while forever blissfully in motion atop the
gentle chop of inshore waves.
For my anchor is not one of galvanized steel
to keep me afloat, but one of breath, blood
and bone.
A mysterious land of which he is King all on
his own allowing few close enough to ever
embrace his shores.
Yet he embraces me.
Places are often no more than the space I
have held for he and his name or his words
that he bleeds, a place of which I ground, no
longer one of a myth-haunted land.
Far more than legends foretold. My anchor.
A safe port of title expressions, a compass
leading only to where the stars are close
enough to finally reach.

JUST ONCE

I don't care where we are in our lives now.
I don't care where we are going to be in our
lives tomorrow.
I simply want the chance to someday look
you in the eyes, holding your hands in mine
for a whole minute.
The chance to know what it feels like to
touch a body that can barely contain the Soul
that lives within it.
To wrap my arms around you, and you I.
Even if only just once.
There are New Worlds out there.
Hold me and give me a chance to show you.

ECLIPSE

The Soul you carry, bleeding out into the
night with every word escaping your lungs
sings the melody of mine. How I long to kiss
those lips and feel your heart beating against
my chest. For this space of proportional
desires, the daydream of possible affairs, is
one of a higher longing that goes beyond
your skin. It's touched far more than all of its
earthly pleasures. If Earth and Water be
opposing signs, I crave ever more the
intimacy in which we both find ourselves
sanely insane pressing into one another and
into the chaos that we are. A healthy affinity
that goes beyond what mere mortals know, a
zenith of mutual understanding impossible
to attain with Air or Fire. Both the axis of
Venus' fall and exaltation, forever exploring
each other and learning. Looking. Seeking.
Reaching. Your analytical mind free of fear
or shame when you let me in to renew your
faith in tangible things your heart desires.
Belief in that you are not fooled. As what's

standing before you not just disrobed, but fully exposed and real. Our acts free from all prejudice to lead wherever they may. When I feel you here, Autumn knocks at my door asking of me to bid the summer farewell. So, I do. For in your pursuit of creating a masterpiece out of everything, I'll be there for you to create one of my flesh and bone. A protection of purity and innocence that others have left open and vulnerable to the wolves. Let your breath be the only thing between us like the Moon between the Sun and the Earth, your lips eclipsing mine.

WARMTH

It's cold outside.
It's cold enough tonight for fleece and
flannel.
Softly wrapping and warming my body.
A welcomed sensation paired with the tea in
hand that I'm sipping.
As I sit and relax, I'm imagining this silky
touch of the cloth I wear is yours.
Soft, warm and safe.
Just as I imagine that every time the hot tea
reaches my lips,
The cup from which it fills, are yours.

UNTIL THE MARKERS RUN DRY

You are worthy of so much love
as you are and where you are.
You are always worth that.
And if on every note I send
I have to tell you until you
believe it, I will run all
of the markers dry until you do.

AS. YOU. ARE.

As. You. Are.
You are enough.
You are good enough.
You've always been good enough.
You will forever be good enough.
This sunrise is for you.

A KING'S HEART & A WOLF'S SOUL

At an hour my eyes should be heavy with
sleep, they are wide and looking up to the
stars beyond these four walls. A longing
behind them, burning to know everything.
Everything beyond your touch, your body; a
privilege to know you that is all mine. To
know more than of your love or the courage
you carry, marked with bands of color in the
tone that you speak when your words part
from your lips. To know more of the bravery
I've not known in another human on this trip
around many suns. Not just that of the
warrior you have been, the battles that
you've seen through to fight for your very
life, but of the wars within you; the darkness
that made you the light that you are. For it is
only those who have risen from the depths
of hell who come back to Earth with such
gentle wings, that shine the way you do. I
want to know every beautiful scar left in the
wake of what burned you. Or to read even a

page from your book, as to do so is to read
the words of love itself. You say you don't
talk about yourself much, yet your art says
so much about you. Opening yourself up in
not only this present space born of your
growth, but from days past. Long before I
knew where you existed in this life. It is in
those early days that I have now listened to
you speak, moments that show the same
Soul but an entirely different human. A
framework being constructed for a healing
guide through pain. You are the very
definition of vulnerability. A courageous act
beyond measure in a world that tears apart
the biggest insecurities of those like you.
Those gallant enough to share them. You are
the definition of Soul. One I feel like I've
always known, yet can't get close enough to.
My body craving to confirm what my heart
already knows, that you are the love in it.
Just as you are a voice for those who cannot
put their own emotions into words to speak
their truths, as you do.

SOMETHING REAL

I've never wanted perfection.
I've wanted something real.
I've never asked for perfection.
But I asked for you.
And you,
you are the most real thing I've ever found.

FOR YOU, SHE WAITS

She's strong-willed.
Dark humored.
Dirty minded.
Sweet and kind.
Soulfully deep.
Vulnerable.
Over the top fucking emotional.
A touch of the dark.
A bright light.
Imperfectly perfect.
Impatiently patient.
Free-spirited yet grounded.
Sometimes impulsive.
The lightest of days.
Your heaviest nights.
Here she waits.
Choosing to stay.
For you.

FIRE MEET FATE

Truth be told I don't care if anyone else sees
me ever again like this. As long as you do.
The only one who will ever see me naked.
Not just physically naked. Something far
deeper. All of my scars. The imperfect
human that I am. Still yearning to learn and
grow to be better each day. What fuels me.
What breaks me. What softens me. All of the
darkness that brought me to the sword I now
wield. A metal forged from every dark
moment, turning each to golden light. Light
that leads me to hope, my truth and to a field
of bluebonnets where my weary head can
now rest full of beautiful dreams. To now see
that I could be far more than they ever said I
would ever amount to be. To be more than
worthy of everything they looked into these
eyes and told me that I never was. I am no
longer afraid. All of the secrets I carry within
this shell now flowing out from this fully
disrobed heart. For only you. I don't know
what the future holds, as none of us do. Only

moments can be known. Day by day. And so, I hold them. All I do know is I'm here now and I'll be here long after you've learned to use your wings to fly again. To find the clouds, with you. No goodbyes. No shutting down in all of the ways I used to in order protect myself from what I truly believed to be an inevitable suffering. A sadness. Another loss. Another moment of not good enough. Another year of laying in a six-foot hole I had already prepared, staring up at the sky waiting to be drown by torrential rain. It ends with openness. Patience. With bravery. With faith. With light and love. And with this fire you've ignited within me just by way of who you are; one that maybe you didn't even know had. And so, the vicious cycle ends for good knowing I carry a sword that this time, I will not fall upon. Instead, using it to keep this path free of the devil and his demons that may try to stand in our way.

ALWAYS CLOSE

Under last night's sky, the stars and its
Moon, I fell asleep looking up; to the thought
of whether or not you had been looking up
at the same view. As you were the ache I felt,
I yearned to know if I was the ache you felt
too. Resting my head upon my arms, my
body wrapped in a blanket upon the grass as
if it had been yours, I closed my eyes. The
bite of cool air to touch my skin leaving
shivers behind. My wanting your warmth
even more; to see the world in that moment
through your eyes. It was then a touch of
warm lips fell upon my forehead, soft and
comforting imploring me to have the
sweetest of dreams. So I dreamt of your face;
of your eyes looking down at me, your Soul
looking into mine. Your sexy fucking Soul.
Of your mouth hovering above mine with
your words being whispered into them
through the darkness, as if to breathe more
life into this still night. Into me. It was the
last thing I remember before I woke to a new

day, to walk through the woods in search of your light again. And I found you in the sunrise, in its beams pushing their way through the staggered trees and their branches; glistening dew upon the pine needles and in between the oaks who have already lost their leaves. It was there I could feel you as if you never left. Always close. I hiked further hoping to catch a glimpse of your face in the essence of the Earth to which your sign belongs. To feel your embrace. To feel what you feel. To see what you see. And to behold all of the energy that is you, to ever reach me. It was then your air filled my lungs through the gentle breeze. You are worth all of the beauty, the chaotic calm and the comfort you bring by simply existing, for me to have found. All of the space your Soul holds with me, worth every moment of the wait; a wait for the day your body can be here too.

SLOW BURN

If it isn't fire and passion, I don't want it.
Inside. Outside. All of it. Consuming. A slow
burn that lasts between visits, in between
sheets, in between conversations, in between
moments of randomness. One that lasts. All
yours. All mine. The adventure. The longing.
The embrace. The connection. Feeling you
feeling me when we are not near. With
patience fueled by a knowing. The
possibility of it being you standing next to
me and laying beside me in the end. Your
hands entwined with mine. Our Souls and
bodies all the same. There to answer every
unanswered question. Yours and mine. To
make the past make sense. To understand all
of the suffering that led to our scars. What it
was all for. Why it was worth it. Together
breathing in deep a single breath; a sigh of
relief. Falling onto you. Into you. Having
you. And you having all of me. Boundless,
endless, with fire and passion. Inside.
Outside. All of it. Consuming. Always.

DREAMS OF EMBRACE

They say it is in the magic of that first kiss that stops time. One of the few things in this life shared between humans that suspends the falling grains of sand in the hourglass; placing them on hold even at mid-fall. Until lips part. A moment. One of many I have often dreamed of sharing, with you. But it's not your lips that rest ever so perfectly upon that smile that lights up everything around it, that I dream of most. It is in all of the art, the absolute magic of your arms and the essence of the Soul to which they belong to, that the dreams of my nights and days crave. The culmination of everything that will have led you to be standing in front of me; sliding your arms underneath my own that first time, pulling me and my heart closer to yours. That moment where time stops will be the one where I can finally rest my head in the middle of your chest; lost in you and your embrace. Not only to feel you, but listen.

GOODNIGHT MOON

May the Moon
and the stars
and your compass
lead you to
beautiful dreams
that continue
when you wake
in the morning
light.

TO BREATHE AGAIN

The few I've let into my heart after he left me
for her always seem to end up afraid to hold
onto me, a tragedy really. Opening the door
only to be let in, cast out, slammed in my
face, pretending I never existed the moment
they realize that I was indeed not too good,
and true. No mystical creature. Just real. An
imperfect human with a light inside of her
that breathes genuine kindness and love. The
forever kind that holds your hand when you
reach for it and never lets it go. The kind
most cannot fathom in a world where bodies
and instant gratification reign supreme. They
forever flee the scene of the crime as the
guilty party, the murderer of beautiful
things. If hearts could be unicorns, call it
mine and pair wings with its golden horn.
I've been too open, too much before. Then
you came along. All of the things I don't
know of you that I want to, I wait to.
Leaving you be when all I want to do is pull
you into me. How you distance yourself

from me, a quiet frustration; like I don't exist
to you when all I want to do is wrap you in
reassurance. To kiss your scars, as they are
mine too. The heart you bleed, your very
essence, mine too. It terrifies me, actually.
I've never known someone like me. A heart
that still hasn't learned when to stop
torturing itself, even after it has been ripped
out of its cage more times than a heart
should and still beat. I should be dead. And
if anyone should have nothing left to give,
no desire to let anyone in, never fall again,
never learn another human again and still
believe in someone loving me the way I
understand love to be, I am the face on that
milk carton. I've kept away every man who
has put out a search party to find me,
begging to become a part of my lonely
world, in the woods. Energy surely does not
lie. I never again thought I would want to
give mine to anyone. But giving to you is
like breathing because I've finally let my
security blanket go, one of fear that had kept
me safe from more of the wrong ones. Those
who know me well know everything I am, a

gift when I feel cursed; an Empath heart
aching for one that matches it. Yours does.

BE BRAVE MOONCHILD

I spent so many years of my young life
trying to fit in, to be what everyone else
wanted me to be.
I wasn't cool enough, pretty enough; well, I
wasn't pretty at all.
And I guess I felt like I didn't even really
exist unless I was being tormented and
bullied, as I was then.
Being at home wasn't any easier unless I
allowed my daydreams to become my
reality, for the first 12 years of my life.
Thinking about it now, I realize why I had
wasted so much of my life trying to convince
other people that I was good enough. When
what I really needed to do was convince
myself I was good enough.
It took years. Decades. Highs. Lows. Abuse
of every kind. Verbal. Physical. Mental.
Emotional. By men who proclaims to care for
our love me. "Friends" too. Users.

And every time I had to convince myself that
I was finally enough, for a time, all it would
take was one person who didn't value me,
one person I wanted to be a part of my life or
to love me to not, to derail it all.
Rejection isn't easy for anyone. But it was
especially hard on me.
It was all I felt I ever knew, for as long as I
could remember.
After finding myself in some of the darkest
places, those that almost ended my life twice
by way of my own hand, I look back at that
terrified little girl; one who felt abandoned
by the world.
At times, she still does.
I hold her in my arms today and tell her how
beautiful she is.
Her imperfections.
Her scars.
I show her how even in the moments she
feels completely alone, that she is a force that
will be okay.
Even on her worst days.
Always one who takes a chance, whether it
be in life or what she craves the most, love.

I tell her that no matter what, to keep being the over-loving heart, the kind soul, fun-loving, adventure seeking traveler, diverse, giving, witty, open and dirty-minded, nonjudgmental, animal loving, free spirit who continues to light every last fire of passion in her matchbox; come rain sleet or snow.

WEAR YOUR HEART LIKE A BEACON

Integrity. It's doing the right thing, even when nobody is looking. And in a world where it continues to become increasingly more difficult to know whose word you can trust, where so many people have ulterior motives and some don't even care who they hurt or step on as long as they cater to their bottom line, it doesn't seem that common anymore. And existing as the "heart on your sleeve" kind, a heart unprotected and more vulnerable to every dagger that exists, even less. For those of us that do, it isn't easy being who we are. All too often, we get taken advantage of because we want to see the best in everyone and genuinely believe they mean what they say and do what they do because they care. I know it might seem hard to believe at times, I struggle with it too. But you are by no means alone in that if these are thoughts and feelings that resonate with you. Just know, there are people who you can trust that don't subscribe to toxic, narcissist, user behavior. One's that have true compassion and care about the feelings and well-being of those outside of themselves. People who live with genuine intentions, mean what they say and act in accordance to those words. Actions speak louder. They are everything. Keep being that light. Let no one dim it or put it out. Keep being that love. Don't let anyone keep you from showing your beautiful heart. Be an example for those who have lost their way. Do so not only for yourself, but for others like us to find one another. We need each other.

PULSE

It's a strange thing.
Being a human who reads energy;
feeling wavelengths of a pulse unrecognized
by most and understanding what they mean.
An innate ability to look into someone's
heart and Soul never having held their hand,
or laying an ear to their heart beating in their
chest.
Of not knowing the small details of their
physical life or body.
Every blemish, every scar. Every eccentricity.
Everything they love or hate about their very
existence; every detail your eyes wish to
behold, your ears want to hear and your
fingers long to trace.
Good or bad, never changing how you feel it
for them.
Sometimes knowing long before they do.
An aura so bright, it's overpowering to my
inner light.
A soulful knowing.
It's a strange thing.

It's that pulse of every color coming together
until they've turned black as night;
making way for the spectacle of electric
waves traveling across the sky like lightning.
You are the sky. They are the lightning.
You feel it everything they've touched and
given to you.
Received by the hands, filling the mind,
embracing your heart down to the soles of
your feet; far deeper than flesh and bone.
Straight from the Earth, and every star that
has ever fallen from the sky.

TAKING NOTES

Intuitive people know when they're being
lied to.
Just because they don't call you out on it,
doesn't mean they don't already know.
It's the ones who remain quiet and calmly
observe that have already taken notes.
They've already put the pieces together long
before you've constructed the lie.
Honesty, much like respect, is priceless in
value; a gift that will never be given by the
cheap.

EVER THINE, NEVER MINE

Whispered in my ear have been their darkest
stories. Of heartache and yearning. Their
fateful path eventually leading to me.
Speaking of magic, of beauty and all of the
amazing things I never knew myself to be.
Others had me believing for so long, that I
was nothing. But there was a beauty in being
nothing; being connected to the knowing
and future hope that I could be something.
Their tales an all-too-familiar dance to a song
these ears can barely make out the words to
anymore. One of their faith in ever finding
the one who carries light wings upon their
shoulders and a golden cup full to the brim
of their heart's blood. Meant only for them.
And forever. Fairy-tales and love's dreams.
That final happy ending where no one runs
or dies; one they lost countless times to
lovers who never knew how to love them.
Giving their all, only for them to leave. So I
love them. Bringing down the very sky, the
Moon and her stars; the heavens themselves

too. Then they leave.

Ever thine, never mine; never knowing what
changes between the good, and goodbye.
Running back to the only stories they know,
clinging to them rather than cling to new life.
Or to me. Living in the pages from a book of
unfortunate things that brought a mind,
body and Soul pain in the 3rd degree. Their
skin unrecognizable without it, while mine
burns away from muscle and bone for such
tales of my own to no longer be a part of me.
No longer giving breath to any wolf that
once huffed and puffed to blow my house
down. Once. Then twice. Fuck my forgiving
heart for letting them blow my house down.

The house that love once built.

It is in these moments and of days like today,
I feel as if I exist in nothing tangible
anymore. But only as pure love standing in
the shadow of hope's fading light. I may not
believe in love the same way I used to when

the dreamer in me, who was too innocent to know any better, was still alive. But that will never be the story I cling to, nor the one I care to continue telling. Even if I am still here, existing only in the back of the mind of another who doesn't want me.

CLOSURE

And then just like that, you were gone again.
But this time the thought of you no longer
hurt me.
I no longer wanted you the way I used to.
And I didn't care about the closure I so
desperately wanted the first time you
disappeared without word.
Like the first time you ignored me.
This time I gave closure to myself.
For you.
And not because you weren't man enough
to.
You just didn't care about me enough to
want to.
It isn't something how ordinary someone
looks after you've decided that they've hurt
you for the last time?

WHERE TRUST DIES

When you're a soul who wants to believe in
the good in everything, everyone,
it's difficult to see the truth at times.
Refusing it. Especially when it comes to love.
And even more so when you see in someone
everything you had been searching for, yet
never found.
Often ignoring your intuition, you'll make all
of the excuses in the world for your heart
and soul's desires. Justifying away how
something really feels at times, in the name
of they being a good person who you believe
would never hurt you like others have.
And with they knowing everything you've
been through, what's been done to you,
you can't believe they would ever allow
themselves to be a repeated cycle in your
life. In any form. Then, they do.
The truth is, someone can have good
intentions, but can't be a good person while
using you and lying to you in order to spare
their own Ego.

One that needs you for everything you have
to give when in its loneliness, to hold it over
while it waits for what it is really looking for
when it knows, you're not it.
I prefer the truth, even if it sucks.
Because being who I am, sooner or later I
always find out the truth and later is always
a million times more hurtful. You can't be a
good person while using others for their
time, energy, money, sex or love, knowing
you are never going to give back anything
that they have so selflessly provided for you
to show you genuine care, love, and take it
anyway. Selfishness in the most simplistic
form.
I've justified. I've rationalized away all of the
excuses to have befallen these ears for those
I've given everything to in the past.
My good heart forever believing in those I let
into it, and that they could never be anything
less than a good person. I rarely ever let
anyone into it, and as this happens to me
more and more, my willingness to do so or
even to trust again, continues to die.
I've been broken again and again by others,

but more so by myself for allowing it.
I've been owed far too many apologies in my
life, ones I've become accustomed to giving
to myself for myself. But also, for them.

GROUNDHOG DAY

And one day, long before your body actually
dies, your light goes out because you've
cried too many tears begging to be free. I've
died too many deaths in this life, my light
snuffed out while I've been left with nothing
to reignite it. Fire and water never mix. But
even when the rain has subsided from my
eyes, they've taken my flint. Forever leaving
me with an endless wooded search for twigs
and sticks desperately grasping at any piece
of dry grass beneath my soles. Enough
kindling to produce even the smallest
promise of smoke and flame. You can fight.
You can reignite your light with next to
nothing left; less and less each time. I've
done it. But the grim reality is that
eventually, all it takes is one final
miscalculated step to send you plummeting
to the bottom of a steep fall. One that won't
kill you, but you'll be numb to the pain after
being beaten by jagged rocks and sharp
stones. The impact will tear the breath from

your lungs in a rush, your mouth agape in shock and gasping for thin air as you look up to the sky with fixed eyes. Shrunken pupils that no longer look at the world or anyone in it the same way because you've learned, nothing is ever as it seems. They say that lightning doesn't strike twice which is an untruth I've come wholeheartedly to know. It strikes more. It strikes over and over again, never producing the blaze I put my all into, yet struggle to build. Instead, it numbs me just enough so that the next time I have to rise from the ashes, the burn hurts just a little bit less and my lungs receive more air than soot. As with everything however, at a cost. The cost of hope, trust and possibility. The cost of ever knowing love in a way I've never had a chance for it to know me. A tragic tale really. One that no matter how brilliant of a writer you are, how much ink you put into attempting to write a new one, it's the tale of Groundhog Day; that perpetual loop in life without love, a circle of hell I can never seem to write myself out of without the devil's hand pulling me back in.

THE HOWL OF A BROKEN HEART

I once learned being ignored, ghosted was
the most horrible feeling.
All of the questions left unanswered while
you sit and think of all of the reasons it was
you. It isn't, but with every moment of
silence that passes, that's where your mind
finds itself. But I was wrong.
The worst feeling is when you finally let go
of your security blanket, fear that you've
wrapped yourself into protect you from all
of the men who will hurt you again, only to
be hurt again.
Believing in someone wholeheartedly
trusting in how they have spoken to you as
they welcomed all of you and your gifts into
their life.
Their words a reflection of everything they
said to you, only to arrive at a line it seems
as if you were nothing more than the secret
they hid.
A woman and her energy that did so much
for them, but now never existed.

The same words used to speak now for
someone else, except for all to see.
You can't help wonder why you are
perpetually only worth breadcrumbs to
people, when you always give whole loaves.
If anyone had been watching me read those
words, the moment I realized I would not to
be "all his" or he "all mine" as he had told me
nights before, I guess I would describe it as
the moment from an old episode of The
Simpsons. One where they slo-mo replay
Mayor Quimby's son on the Jumbotron the
very moment his heartbreaks, the exact
moment possibility fell from my eyes;
my lips still and silent, agape.
A distinct and hasty exit of all hope, desire
and love before it ever truly knew me.
Before it and he ever held me.
A confirmation of me not being worth
enough to commit to.
I stare now at the trees as I write this, feeling
as hollow as some of them are.
A quiet breeze moving through everything
green that basks in the sunlight of today.

I wonder what it feels like to do that, never
having to wonder if it has room to cover
you each day it shines. Knowing it will come
back even if hidden by clouds,
a constant that chooses to stay focused on
the world loving it, until the day it dies;
as all stars someday do.
Enough to ever feel safe to be vulnerable
again, to give your all to anyone,
ever again.

JUST THE HOOKER

It's really difficult to believe that you are
enough at times.
Deep down you know you are but when no
one ever wants to give you a real chance
over something more instantly gratifying,
difficult to do some days.
The difficulty lies in that being, the story of
your life is that you are perpetually either
the friend that people are so blessed to have
because you're the one who is always there
to do so much, even when it's not
reciprocated; or you're just the emotional
and physical hooker paid only by the hope
that maybe it will be different. Just once.
But you're never more than an option. A
second choice. A question mark.
A maybe instead of a fuck yes.
A completely undesirable slow burn that
would last until your final breath,
but can in no way be any match for an
instant flame.
It isn't easy being thoughtful and genuine in

this world thinking about others all the
time when most people you think about
every day, probably haven't given you a
single thought.
It isn't easy being a white lighter; the white
heart that I have always carried within me.
It isn't easy being love itself while craving it,
only to never receive it.
I don't know why it still shocks me when the
love I give is not enough for someone to
want more of it from me, to share in it with
me.
Because no matter how warm and inviting I
am, no matter how vulnerable, giving,
selfless and whatever other adjectives that
have been used by others to describe me, I'm
still here completely alone.
Worth no distance, no time, no weight, no
commitment or even simply a fair shot;
and never have been for anyone in my
journey in this life. Truth, I have no one.
Happiness is a butterfly.
I could lie to you and tell you everything is
okay all the time but it wears on you,
eroding a positive mindset faster than ice
melting on a hot summer day.

A repeated lesson that starts to harden you;
this white heart of mine, well on its way to
turning completely black.

NOTHING MORE

I am forever a child of the Universe's Cosmic
cruel joke.
A place on a map seemingly lost,
yet people still find a me to stop for a while.
Even if only to rest their weary eyes for a
moment to dream,
and fill their bellies before leaving.
A brief pause.
Nothing more than a stopping point between
where they started and love,
that isn't mine.

THE JOKER

I've known many men to sit before me on a
thrown of lies; poetic words to my eyes and
ears that befall me empty, with false promise
just to keep my energy near. Intentions
match only their of a lack of action, yet it has
taken me until now to accept the many
truths I've made excuses for in the past, just
to hold them close in any way that I could.
And for no other reason than maybe because
my eyes could not stand to behold another
familiar scene. Each consequential one far
more cunning than the last; a con of this very
heart and Soul. But it is not others who hath
fooled my intuition or the very Empath that I
am, one that holds steady, loyal and true to
seeing the good in everyone and everything.
It is in this hindsight of the chaos of you that
I find clarity. Absolution. For it was never
me nor them, but the unhealed anger you lie
to yourself about that will see you to the
same end, every time. The thing that can

only be hidden for so long before breaking
free of the chains you fight to keep them in
so no one will see it. One cannot be a fraud
to the world for long, any more than they
can be the joker to themselves. I allowed you
to fool me. I allowed you to use me. I invited
you in to start a fire that would burn too hot,
too fast and inevitably, burn down to
nothing but moments of my existing at your
convenience; in your world among other
secret women come forth as they no longer
hide behind your false promises. I wonder
what you offered them. What they gave to
you. And then again, I don't as it's probably
similar in story; running along the lines of
the same wheel you turned in rotation
between us all. Selfishness disguised by
selflessness, a concern for them as I, that
never existed. All about, you. We being
nothing more than beautiful pawns in an
endless game. One of which I will never
again touch upon the board as I stand strong
walking away from it, not a pawn, but a
fucking Queen.

GOODBYE LIES & COULD HAVE BEENS

My eyes saw you. My ears heard you. My
Soul felt yours. My heart wanted to love
yours.
My body wanted to be with yours. But now
your words linger like daggers stuck in these
walls as words do nothing to quiet these
bones. At least within the confines of this
darkness, they're numb to you now.
If I was brave enough to behold one now,
maybe I would remember what it was like in
those moments to feel anything other than
this. But maybe it's better that I don't.
My wings have already turned, light feathers
scattering somewhere below me to make
room for heavier ones amidst the reality that
I've had to face. A truth that has emptied my
eyes and shattered these bones more than
once before; ending the very life of what
remained within them, each time I've given
my all to anyone who had no intention of
giving me theirs. Yet they keep pieces of

them anyway for their selfish needs, only to
scatter each fragment as I watch when no
longer needed. One by one turned to ash and
swept away by the wind; written off as if I
did nothing; was nothing, am nothing.
The raven's words, these daggers, the closest
I will ever be to you or your love.
Your eyes don't see me. Your ears don't hear
me. Your Soul doesn't feel mine.
Your heart never wanted to love mine. And
your body used mine until it wanted to be
with someone else. At least now I can go to
bed unafraid of these walls, for I am in
the comfort of heartache's familiarity.
With no more bones left to break nor
feathers to lose, I am able to let go of the
what could have beens that never wanted to
be.

TIPPING SCALES

Grief is simply the price we pay for Love.
Is it worth it?
One million times over.
Yes.
Because having love at all is worth it.
The pain of its loss may never fully go away,
but you grow stronger because of it.

ENOUGH TO BURN

You have to get to a point when enough is
enough.
When someone isn't burning enough for you
to want to burn with you, learn to burn for
yourself.
Be your own fire.

THEY ALWAYS COME BACK

You lost me.
And you can never have me again.
You can never have what we had again.
You neglected me.
You ignored me.
You made me feel less.
You made me feel like there was someone else.
You skirted around your own fears.
Tiptoed around me. How you felt about me.
Denying yourself the chance for us.
I gave you everything.
Showed you everything.
You gave me nothing.
The easiest way to lose me.
For good.
My Soul I bared to you in complete trust.
Looking at you through rose colored glasses.
I made excuses for you.
For your excuses to me.
But now I see.
You used me.

Neglected me.
Ignored me.
Took away your attention.
Took away your affections.
Took away your reassurance.
Took me for granted.
My very forgiveness for granted.
Take. Take. And take some more.
Giving it to others you didn't even know.
Never again will I hear your apologies.
Never again will I walk through your door.
I do forgive you.
But you can't ask.
You can't beg or plead.
You lost me.
A lesson to them.
A lesson to you.
And anyone else who doesn't want to lose
me too.

I SETTLED FOR YOU

You once told me that I was deserving of
everything.
And that you hoped I never settle for less.
But I did. I settled for less to show you there
was more out there.
Genuine and real.
The kind you don't have to ask for.
And I guess in doing so my role in that was
to show you love and how to be open to love
again.
But with someone else.
I settled for you.
I will never settle again.

JUST ENTERTAINMENT

If you would have given me the chance to
love you,
to feel and receive all that you longed for
and missed in your life,
you would have known my love forever.
But with you, I then had to face the most
difficult truth of all.
That I was once again nothing more than
someone's entertainment while they looked
for something more.

THE STRUGGLE

When you've spent much of your life having
to guess where people stand in it, if they
even do as they've come and gone so many
times before, you appreciate so much more
the ones who open up to tell you exactly
how they feel for you. To never have you
guessing. To so intimately bleed your own
heart before another takes a strength not
known by many. It's easy to love. But to be
vulnerable enough to express it, the most
difficult part of all.
The struggle to tell people what they mean
to our very Soul, is not innate. Albeit natural
for some humans to have a more timid
nature, the fear of vulnerability is shaped by
negative experiences we have had
throughout our lives. As are most things,
psychologically speaking. To this day, I find
it easier to write how I feel for someone;
intended for them to know my heart in those

words. I've gotten better, where expressing
my love is not only heard, but seen, felt,
reciprocated. Those who have left us when
we wanted nothing more than for them to
see us as we saw them and to stay, often the
reasons why we pass by the future chance to
fully open ourselves to anyone new, again.
Fearing the same outcome. I swore I would
never, but here I am unwilling to pass up the
right one. Humans have this insane
capability of talking ourselves out of
everything from the best things for us to the
greatest possibilities of our lives and often, in
love. A coping mechanism of protection for
our already bruised, sometimes fragile
bones. And for something we have not yet
tapped the full potential of, this brain within
our skulls is able to do such a disservice to
us. Case and point of my life. A handful of
times; some by way of undeserved second
chances. Sometimes they're great to give, but
all too often when it comes to love they are
just a reminder of how fucking stupid our
hearts can be at times. Masochists in a sense.
The only thing willing to do and give more,

to get less. Mine loves hard. It always has. It is a forgiving & giving thing. Something I've had to hold back countless times in my life; my raw intensity and genuine emotion too much for some. Truth be told, a rare thing in the world and I say this humbly so, their loss. I can't tell you how I got to this point where being vulnerable became a more acceptable part of me than being a demon I fought with every day. But now, I don't hold back. I take the chances to say or do everything. And simply because, that despite this illusion of immortality we all carry within us while making future plans for our lives, tomorrow is never promised. And if I am to leave this world, I don't want to leave it never knowing.

GAMES ARE FOR BROOMSTICKS

She grew tired of the games.
So, she just stopped playing.
The harsh reality humans really don't like to
admit to themselves is that most people
don't care about you, for real.
They only care about what you can do for
them, what you can provide to fulfill their
needs.
And once you've stopped giving what it is
that you supply, you find out pretty quickly
because they will mystically disappear.
Some vocally making it all about them before
bowing out, never taking note of the
behavior or lack thereof that caused you to
stop.
But you will find those genuine souls who
want to see you succeed, who reciprocate on
the same level and even if you are a total
stranger to them.
More often than not, total strangers you
might connect with in some way, want to see
you win more than your own family, friends,

spouses or significant others.
Those people, in competition with no one
but themselves.
And you can't compete with confident,
strong individuals who know what they
bring to the table.
They are the ones who want to see you win,
maybe even offering you a seat at their table.
The world is full of games no matter what it
is in life, love and everything in between.
It is simply up to you to decide which ones
are worth playing.
For me, games belong on football fields, in
hockey rinks and on broomsticks chasing
Quidditch balls.

IN THE SHADOW OF HINDSIGHT

Humans will speak the most positive words,
insightful and sometimes cliche when they
find themselves at the height of happiness.
High off of the newness set to release the
surge of dopamine and serotonin, it's easy to
preach optimism and faith when it is
presently coursing through your veins.
This is simply how we are wired, our body's
reaction to the fulfillment of our lifelong
desires.
We project it onto others. Even when it is the
last thing that some of them may need to
hear in that moment, of their darkest hour.
So soon do we forget what it is like to be in
that space; one that in between rounds of
happiness and love, we have all been.
And when you are standing in the grace of
the light you've been seeking for so long,
the shadow of hindsight always stands near
as a vehicle for rationalization.
A way to carve some deeper meaning out of
your suffering that has long since passed,

to make sense of it all; a sense of balance
between the truth and something deeper that
we all we crave in life. Something we have to
dig deep and fight for even if it's not reality.
Sometimes it does. Sometimes it doesn't. Yet
there are always lessons to be learned.
I look back at all the times I felt exactly this
way and how every time I believed that my
suffering was finally coming to an end. That
chemical relief, that knowing, that heart,
Soul and gut feeling; everything I felt I had
then, a product of my irrevocable belief in
the goodness we give to others coming back
to us tenfold.
In part, that notion that keeps me blindly
giving when all others do is take from me.
When our cups are full and overflowing
with happiness, we sing its chorus to all who
will listen.
We pray it remains. We pray that this time it
never leaves. I hope for everyone who
believes this way, it doesn't. In those
moments in my life, I never believed it
would but always ended abruptly;
even when I still believed in some path to

my biggest dream.
Some would call it blind faith. I just call it
faith.
As I know all too well, that the only thing
truly blind is love.
Because when you have it, and a magnificent
back-story from where you started to where
you are now to give more meaning to it, it
quickly becomes the answer to your biggest
prayers. There are stories of my own, such as
these, I have told a few times before. You
become a beacon for all who suffer still,
a sense of hope even if for some, it is a false
one. And if one day the happy chemicals that
go along with it are stripped away, whether
what you asked for stayed but changed over
time as all things do or it simply leaves for
something else; you'll no longer be blinded
by it even though you have just been
blindsided by it. It is in those moments you'll
know what was real.
Only then, will you know your hope is real.
Your character, your truth, your strength.
None of it will ever be found in a person's
greatest joy or in the fulfillment of one's

deepest desires any more than it will be
found in the most comfortable places. For it
is found in the times that break all
your bones, rip out your heart, burning you
to the very ground on which you stand, only
to leave you for dead.
And if you find yourself still singing that
chorus for all to hear then,
that is a true testament to who you are and
how real your faith really is.

THE DREAM OF FOREVER

These days it's difficult to keep the faith in
ever finding not just someone who knows
what love is, but one who wants to share it
with me. To stay. Build a beautiful life with
me. Complement each other's existence.
To want to know everything about me with
the enthusiasm, I have for them;
bordering obsession where you just can't
know enough of every part.
Finding beauty in flaws, scars and to be
there to caress them until they are
nothing short of works of art. And not just
on the good days, the bad too.
Pages of forever good mornings and good
nights. To want to give everything.
Receive everything. Equally.
Someone I don't have to teach how to treat
me or make me feel special.
I am in no way complicated. It's all about
affection, caring, desire and mutual embrace.
One where I'm truly all theirs, they mine,
and it is just natural because they too know

what it's like to not be reciprocated. Adored.
Craved. Loved to the bone, from the inside
out.
In all of the ways nobody else ever did.
I've only crossed paths with one Soul like
that in my entire life recently, and briefly.
But no matter how much I gave and showed,
it wasn't enough for it to be me in the end.
Not that I wasn't good enough. I honestly
don't know what it was. Timing maybe, who
knows.
But he healed my heart, some. Showed me
what I need. I was willing to stay, made it
clear I was there, always close. There to
show him just how special he was.
A gift even though it hurts to never have had
a real chance with him; the silver lining in it,
I know wholeheartedly what's necessary for
me to open my heart again.
But a terrifying thing all the same because
humans like us are some of the rarest in
existence.
We are far more Soul than anything else.
Knowing what I need, what I deserve,
I didn't know truly existed in the world

before him. Comforting in one sense of the breath, but hopeless in another. As I know that you can have a strong connection with someone in nearly every way, but it does not mean they are going to choose you and stay. The thing that happens to most after the infatuation period has burned off due to diving into intensely, headfirst into anything. A hard lesson I have learned many times in my life; the anxiety and fear accompanying that weighing heavily on me tonight.

I know all I can do now is focus on myself again. Heal even more. But it has been over a decade of my doing so; me being irrevocably ready more so in the last five years than ever, for someone to share my life with me.

I just hope that the next time I'm not looking and someone shows up, I don't have to lose them to someone else. That they just know. Because sadly, that's all I know.

From losing my high-school sweetheart to a "close friend," losing the man I married to my "best friend" after 13 years, the next to Lord knows what but probably another woman, to the next I never even had a real

chance with before he met someone else.
Sure, I'm hellfire when it comes to falling
and rising again, but I'm human too. And life
is far too short, I'm getting too old and I've
never known truly what it is like to be loved
the same as I love.
The ache has grown stronger, the
culmination of five years of growth and
learning how to love and live solely for
myself in a way I've never done before.
If I had to choose one thing on my bucket list
that I cannot leave this world without, it
would not be the desire of most wanting to
see some great monument or canyon. Albeit,
I do want to see so much of this beautiful
world, it would be far more for me to
experience that kind of love.
I would give up everything for that dream.
It is the reason life itself on Earth exists.
So here I am, moving forward in hopes that
my forever finds me, and stays.

SOMEDAY

Maybe someday,
is all we can ever really
hope for.

SHE

She's not the one you
light fires for.
She's the one you burn
with.

THE ART OF THE RELEASE

This year, I'm going back to putting my all
into me.
I've lost myself twice in the last two years
putting my all into people in the name of
what seemed like divine meddling in my
life; a meant to be.
The meant to be's showing up at my door to
let themselves in, only to steal all of the
furniture on the way out. One final and very
important lesson to drive home the point of
my holding close my energy, time, money,
all that I am and no longer giving so freely in
the hopes that it will be reciprocated by
those who have no intent or desire to do so.
No more listening to words.
This year is all about action. There's toward
me. Mine for me.
And for anyone who comes along wanting to
not only be a part of my life, but for anyone
who values me at all.
I've allowed too many in who at the end of
the day, speak empty words; caring less

about me versus what I could do for them.
A hard pill to swallow, but one of truth.
Well, this year, no more.
And albeit the saying is as played out and
tired as telling people to "love yourself and
be your own best friend," something I've
learned to do a long time ago or I wouldn't
still be alive or moving forward in my life,
I have to believe what is meant for us will
come. But what's more, stays.
The only certainty I have is that I am meant
for me.
And as I start this new season in my life am
attached to no one, but me.
I will never change in my strength and
resilience, even when the darkness
looms over me, nor will my brutal honesty
disappear to make anyone more
comfortable. I am always a safe space, but
one that will never lie to you.
This heart and Soul of mine, they will
forever remain the same beautiful and kind
things that they have always been, even as
this mind and body continues to grow and
change. It's all far less about what is "meant

to be" or "loving yourself."

It's more so about learning to release the ties
that bind you, leaving dead things
remembered, but free to rest where they lay.

THE LIE THAT IS TIME

Time. It is no legitimate measure of anything here. A man-made illusion created to fool ourselves into thinking there is always going to be more of it. But it is not the creator of bonds or the connector of energies. And it does not heal all wounds any more than the amount of it that comes to pass is a measure of what's real. It is the people, places and things that have reached inside your heart with such depth that are the true measure. The most priceless. It is in the places so memorable that even with age the experience will never be erased from your mind. The taste of the air, the sounds, the sights, the smells. But above all the truest measure is what we share and who we share with. And it is with those rare souls that have spoken to us in all the ways others may have not spoken to us before. All the ways we needed to hear and sometimes, in the ways we did not. It is those that have placed their hand to our chests, reaching inside to

touch even the darkest parts of us, unafraid
of our scars. The love and light not deterred
by one's darkness; a darkness we all carry
within us. Time does not cause one to open
up. Time does not cause one to heal.
Connection does. That Soul-to-Soul
connection. These things are a true measure.
As it is in those rare connections, that even to
they who are the most broken or maybe at a
time when you are at your most broken too,
that will remain the most beautiful thing you
will ever behold. A true measure of
everything. Breathe in deep and behold them
in every way that you can, while you can.
This all ends someday.

REGRETS

If you are to be anything,
be brave.
Hold nothing back.
Regrets are only words unsaid.
And actions left undone.
But the consequences of each,
will go with you to the grave.

SUNDAY MORNING

Hold close those who not only understand
you and all that you are, but who Love
unconditionally. Every piece of you, finding
buried treasures in your scars. Those who
support you even on the days that you are
incapable of doing either for yourself. They
are a rarity in this world. Those who deserve
us are not the ones that can provide the most
in physical or monetary favor. It's the ones
or one who delight in your sheer existence,
every day showing you how much your
spirit means in this world, and in theirs. You
will know them as they will find the most
joy in your smile and radiance in your
sunshine. Yet be courageous in navigating
your storms, capturing every tear to hold
before you and turn into diamonds.
Someone who cannot love you at your worst,
does not deserve you at your best. And the
one who does, will wake up next to you
every beautiful Sunday morning bewitched
by the tangled mess of the perfectly

imperfect bodies that brought your Souls
together. Finding your hands to interlace
their fingers with yours in acknowledgment
and appreciation of all that you are now and
ever will grow to be. And they will grow
with you, never once entertaining the option
of letting go of your hand.

REMARKABLE

You are nothing short of remarkable.
All you have overcome.
All that you are.
As you are.
And I am forever grateful to be here,
for all of you.
Never forget that.

UNCAGE YOUR HEART

And this is my wish for you today,
that you don't hold back in your life.
If it scares you, that you try.
Try with everything that you are.
All that you have within you.
Uncage your Heart.
Find a warmth you've never known.
One that goes above and beyond all others.
Not just for now, but for a lifetime.
Open your heart to the possibilities of what
could be,
fully letting go of what was.
What never again will be.
Because what's coming is better than what's
gone.
It might already be standing before you.
Waiting for you to call it your own.
Stake your claim.
Yours. All yours.
Because what's yours is waiting for you to
reach for it.
Grab it by the hands and pull it into you.

Pull it in close enough to inhale everything
that it is or ever could be.
To not just see it or feel it, but taste it.

For More Writings & Books to Come,
Visit: www.CynthiaLee.org

Follow *Cynthia Lee* on Instagram @_cynthia.lee
Personal Blog @cynthiaeternal

www.ingramcontent.com/pod-product-compliance
Lightning Source LLC
Chambersburg PA
CBHW021229090426
42740CB00006B/449